ALL CRACKED UP

PRESTON ALFONSO SCOTT, SR.

Copyright © 2023 Preston Alfonso Scott, Sr.
All rights reserved
First Edition

NEWMAN SPRINGS PUBLISHING
320 Broad Street
Red Bank, NJ 07701

First originally published by Newman Springs Publishing 2023

ISBN 978-1-63692-773-2 (Paperback)
ISBN 978-1-63692-774-9 (Digital)

Printed in the United States of America

This book is dedicated to my loving mother, Margaret. She's raised me in church and to always do the right thing! Also in remembrance to my four nieces and one nephew who lost their lives.

Lives in Muskogee, Oklahoma. Massacre gone too soon, Feb 2, 2021

Jackpot—The woman of my dreams, a strong and beautiful Black woman who I love so dearly! But because of my anger, due to long-distance relationship, I've lost her! I pray that someday, I will win her love back. Love her forever.

The story outlined in this book is in no way to glorify the use of crack cocaine but simply to express how it destroyed my life! Nor does it intend to take away any pain from trauma of any of the women that had children during our relationship and the victims whose lives I encountered throughout this journey.

Born on August 23, 1957, in Los Angeles General Hospital to the proud parents of my father, Samuel Andrew Scott, and mother, Margaret Clayton! Lived in the projects, Nickerson Gardens, in Watts on the corner of Imperial Highway and Central Avenue. Moved away from there to my mother's hometown of Muskogee, Oklahoma, after the 1965 Watts riot! Back then, it was Jay Hawk Burgers. Hamburgers were $0.25, and cheeseburgers were $0.35! After moving to Muskogee to Thirteenth Street, we lived across the street from my Uncle Emry, and up the street lived my grandpa and grandma! Enrolled in Dunbar Elementary School in the second grade. Being new kids in the neighborhood, well, we had to fight! This city was small and racists! All the White people lived on one side of the track, and us Black folks lived on the other side of the tracks. My first fight after school, I came home crying! I didn't fight back. That was a no-no! My big brother Bobby and my cousin Johny took me in our backyard and kicked my butt but made me fight back. What they do that so, back to school, my second fight was at the Dairy Mist Candy Store. This was where everyone hung out after school. Now, mind you, across the street from Dunbar was Saddler Junior High School! And up the hill was Manual Training High School. The Dairy Mist is where all the after-school fights took place. My time to shine! I picked a fight with Reggie; he liked a girl I liked named Cee Cee! She had to be mine! Reggie had a reputation for being a good fighter. So when we put the sticks on our shoulders, that's how we started out fighting.

"Knock mine off."

"No, you knock mine off."

So I did! I fought with my head down and my eyes closed. All I could remember was my big brother and cousin telling me, "Open your eyes. And you better not come home crying again." When I opened my eyes, I saw I was winning. Well, I turned into Cassius Clay! And Cee Cee became my first girlfriend. Fighting became my trademark after school. All the girls like me, and the guys hated and were afraid of me!

On Twelfth Street were some older boys that my mother told me to stay away from. They became my best friends. They had horses and BB guns. I became a cowboy. I had to show them I could fight to hang with them and steal! Out of the bunch, Victor became my best friend—until we snatched a purse from an elderly White women who was eighty-one years old and drugged her up the alley! She wouldn't let go of her purse. She almost died! They made us visit her in the hospital, touch her, and beg her forgiveness! Then we were sent to the boys' home! Victor went to Hellena because he was fifteen. I went to Boley because I was thirteen. We got separated, and we both cried! Now I'm on my own, and I gotta be tough! You had to be nine years old to fourteen years old to be at Boley Juvenile Hall. First day there, you had to prove yourself worthy! So I picked a fight and got thrown in solitary confinement for ten days! I was so afraid. The house father kept me afloat!

Mr. Hightower said to me, "So you like to fight. After your ten days are up, you still wanna fight! Then you can sign up to fight in the gym every weekend. Just pick anybody."

Boley was in the country, and they had their own dairy. We had duties. I was chosen to milk cows. It was fun! Every morning at three o'clock, we had to round up our assigned cows and have them milked by six o'clock before breakfast! Every weekend, I had to have at least three fights. They gave us gloves and a face mask. If you wore it, you were considered a punk. I never did! Then we had tournaments against other boys' home; it was great! I wanted to be a pro fighter! Then I met Mr. James. He was our barber! He was cool! Now I wanna be a barber! Then basketball season started. I signed up for that and became a starter. I patterned my game after Earl "The Pearl" Monroe, and I shot and scored just like him.

Now I was back home from Boley boys' home after nine months' stay! I never wanted to leave. I ate better and lived better even though my mother had her own garden in the backyard. We were poor. Commodities from government were cheese, potatoes, and beans! My mother made it work. I considered my mom being a slave; she scrubbed floors and washed White folks' clothes! There was a time in 1968 where they hung three of my mother's brother Ike's best friends for speaking to a White girl.

Back to 1971, after returning from Boley! Color TVs had just came out. They started integration. We are going to be bussed across the tracks to Patricia Robertson Junior High School, mixed with the White kids! Here we go! It was some twins who lived up the streets from me—George and Gorden Chandler. They had five sisters and four brothers: sisters Letha, Tina, Wanda, Patrica, and April and brothers Paul, Elijah, Horace, and Tim. They were two years older than me, and I looked nothing like them. But we all dressed alike as triplets. Now as you continue to read, you will figure out where the name Peekaboo comes from. Let me take you back to when I was in the third grade at Dunbar!

My math grade teacher's name was Mrs. Booth! And she had a booth for me for sure. I like dropping my pencil and looking under girls' dresses, it gave us fellows something to laugh and tease about. Mrs. Booth had what she called time-out! Since I was the class clown, I often was made to stand in a corner facing the wall!

One day, Mrs. Booth said, "You like looking under dresses."

She put me under her desk, blocked the front of the desk, and made me sit there and look under her dress! If I was to move, she would kick me. She had the prettiest white panties I had ever seen. But what was different about looking under her dress! She was hairy as the afro I had on my head. She wore this sheer stockings that was see-through, and she had these hairy legs and a mustache! I would forever pursue hairy women! There were these two girls in my class;

both first names were Regina. After recess, they would call me by the girls' restroom and raise up their dress, then laugh, and put them back down. Plus, they were a little hairy. So now every day after school, I would chase them home. We all were on the school's track team. I was one of the fastest boys, and they were some of the fastest girls.

Let the fun begin! Catch me, and you can get it! Let's start with Regina number one! She lived on the south side of town, and I had to chase her up a hill and then down the hill. Man, she was fast. Now I would always agree to a head start.

On your mark, get set, ready, go! She always cheated, starting on "get set"! I was determined to catch her! One day, running down the hill, I caught her; and we tumbled and fell. I ended up on top of her.

She started to cry. "Please, I can't have sex, but you can touch it and kiss me."

As far as I was concerned, that was having sex. We were nine years old! Now Regina number two. She was a different story and much faster! Her best friend was Gena Lola; she would do the count! I chased her too, but when I caught her, she would fight. Anyway it took two weeks to catch Regina number two! She would cheat also, and she had to take her house key to open the door. She beat me, locked the door, then opened it naked and teased me! I had to have her. So one day, Gena Lola started counting. Now Regina had a head start too! When she said, "Get set," I started too. Regina tried to close the door! I stepped my foot in there just in time, then my whole leg. Regina started to cry!

I told her, "Old know, we had a deal."

She cried, "Please, my mama be home in a minute. But you can touch it and kiss me!"

Then she closed the door and laughed and teased me butt naked and called me a dummy. We became best friends after that. She would always let me catch her so we could rub and kiss. Until one day, we got caught by her mother!

Back to me and the twins' first day at integrated school dressed as triplets! Our mothers told us not to let them little White boys beat us at anything—in the class or at sports! That meant to us fighting too. Guest who started the riot at lunch in the cafeteria? We did! Since I passed the first punch, I was kicked out of school for the whole year! Got my butt whipped, first by my mother, then my grandma, and, last but not least, my grandpa. Believe it or not, he was the coolest! Back then, you had to pick your own switch from the tree or bushes. I caught myself picking a small one. My little brothers and sisters would go out at Mom's request and bring back a tree limb!

Then they would later tease and laugh at me about it. I was next to the oldest of six—four boys and two girls! They all were Andersons, and I was the only Scott! So my mom's enrolled me in an all-Black school in Tullahassee, Oklahoma, about twelve miles from Muskogee. If you thought Muskogee was country, then Tallahassee was more country. I had to walk and catch a ride every day to Shawnee Highway! This street took you in and out of the city of Muskogee both ways north and south!

First day of school in ninth grade, fifteen years old with nothing to prove, I focused on all the pretty young straight country girls! First guy I met, his name was Lesley. He asked me if I could play ball. I said yes! He took me straight to Coach Newton! The gym had the looks of a barn, and it only could seat a mere fifty people. The school was made up entirely on one building that consisted of all grades. From the first grade to the twelfth. The eighth-grade girls were all on me. Fresh meat! There were Tookie and Arjane in particular! Tookie played for the girls' team, and Arjane was a cheerleader. The girls practiced on one half of the gym, and us boys on the other half. Tookie and Arjane had the prettiest legs I had ever seen! Lesley told me Tookie had a crush on me. He hooked us up. She was so shy! By this time, I had already experienced sex by then. Tookie was a virgin and afraid. She played hard to get, so we broke up! And I went after Arjane! I became a starter on the team, and I had brought me a 1961 Chevy station wagon for $300.00! That was me and the twin's sex mobile! I took them to my games and to meet them country girls. Everybody loved twins, but you couldn't keep us triplets apart. They had to love me too! We would take turns in the wagon! Tullahassee had the look of farm and country all around us. Most houses were at least four blocks apart. At our basketball games, the White boys' only way to keep me from scoring was to call me a nigga! The coaches knew I would lose my cool and start a fight, with my twin brothers to back me up. So I ended up kicked out of school again and back to the Boley boys' home! Patrica and April were the youngest sisters of my twin brothers, and Elijah was the babe boy!

Patrica and April both used to take turns braiding my hair! They were a year apart, and April was two years younger than me. But they were fine. Patrica loved to tease me, tongue kiss me, and let me feel and grind on her. Then when we got ready to have sex, she would love to say, "Stop, you are my brother." I wanted to disown the twins; they even said they were my sisters! April teased me. When she would braid the front of my head, she always had a dress on, kept her legs wide open, let me look at it, but slapped me on the head whenever I touched it.

Couldn't get along with my stepfather! My mama thought I had ran away from home! So she visited Mama Chandler, and I became officially part of the family. I would only go down the hill to my mama's house to eat and slept in the back house with the twins and Elijah! I fell in love with Trica and April, but I had to accept we could tease and play but no sex because I had become part of the Chandler family! Oh yeah, almost forgot about Gene. He was the oldest. I began to meet the rest of the family. I had a crush on the oldest sister, Letha, too! They all treated me as their sibling, little brother from another mother!

My first virgin girlfriend, Patricia Faye! Being with the twins, I had plenty of girlfriends, but Patricia was a virgin. While in Boley boys' home, she had sex with Elijah, the twins' youngest brother. I was hurt; it could have been anybody but my brother. A child was conceived, and to this day, I still don't know if I'm the father! Then there was Barbara, who wrote me while I was in Boley and was my girlfriend and whom Elijah married and had children by after being released from Helena instead of Boley!

As I had mentioned earlier, I tried to return to my mama's house, only to find out how badly my stepfather had been beating my mother. Notice I said my mother! I am the black sheep of the family but now the oldest because my older brother Bobby had been shipped to the air force! I had previously brought my mother a gun, and we kept it hidden under the front room couch! So when my stepfather blocked the door and wouldn't let me into the house, I asked my mama where my suitcase was at. She stated behind the couch, and I knew exactly what she meant. I jumped behind the couch, grabbed the gun, pointed it at him, and told him to get out of my mama's house!

He started toward me saying, "Give me the gun, little boy."

My mama was yelling, "Shoot him in the leg!"

She saved his life! I shot him in the leg. We all jumped and got into my mama's Toyota two-door car. He ran screaming into the back room.

Mama, a little tipsy, was saying, "My babies and I all on the run. Let's get out of town."

I was a juvenile, and I stated, "No, Mama, we are going to the police station, and I will tell them what happened."

They couldn't question my younger brothers and sisters; they were minors. I was three months from being eighteen years old. I told them it was an accident and he tried to take the gun from me and, when I pulled back, he got shot in the leg. I took a lie detector test. Passed it or not, I was released to my mama the same day. Case closed. Record sealed. Remember, my mama ironed these people's clothes and washed them on her hands. There wasn't such a thing as a washing machine by then. But my probation officer wanted to send me back to Helena for use of a firearm! I ran, and my mama and uncle put me on a Greyhound to live with my mama's younger sister Lorene!

My Aunt Lorene and her husband, Ed, were having marriage problems; so I ended up moving in with my mama's younger brother Ike! Ike was a Vietnam vet; he worked as a mailman. His wife, Nette, the same age as me, was a housewife. And we became close, and I dated her baby sister Pat! Ike and Nette fought a lot, and I always tried to intervene. Then I was accused of having sex with her. So I was kicked out!

Lucky for me, I had a car and a job. I worked as a busboy at ABC Super Market on Fifty-Fourth and Main. I found myself a room for rent on top of Jimmy Furniture Store on Fifty-First and Main. I hit the nightlife and started clubbing and pop-locking in dance contests. I worked the seven-to-four shift; and being nineteen years old in 1976, I would leave the clubs at two in the morning, get a few hours of sleep, then go to work at seven! I eventually started stealing on my job when people couldn't pay for their large amount of food. One of the cashiers, Jeanie, would throw me her keys and tell me to put that food in the trunk of her car. During the holidays, Thanksgiving and Christmas, my family on my mama's side loved me. Turkey and hams, I supplied them all.

A year later, I got busted. I was fired and moved to Inglewood and got a job at Boy's Market! Moved into this hotel called the Imperial Hotel right next to the Imperial West Night Club! I could pass for twenty-one years old; they let me in because I could dance! Got tight with the DJ Moonman and became his sidekick! The hotel and club was on the corner of Imperial and Parle. There was a McDonald's on Century and Parle down the block. This was where I met Darlene; she worked at McDonald's. We dated about three months. She told me one day she was pregnant. I told her I didn't believe, and I had never seen or heard from her again. That's another story!

Back at the Imperial Hotel, it was full with hookers! They were everywhere! I met one named Nicole. She liked me and would give me free sex to watch her back. It caught on. Until now, I was getting a lot of sex from a lot of hookers to watch their backs! I and Nicole, we had signals when things were going wrong. One night, she gave that signal, and I kicked the door in. This guy, butt naked, was choking and fucking her at the same time! It was a dog chain on the dresser.

So I grabbed it, and he faced me and said, "What you gonna do with that?"

I beat his ass, first across his private part, but wore him out! The police came. He pressed charges and said we tried to rob him, lured him into the room, and attacked him. We went to jail for battery and robbery. Three days later, DA rejected; we were both released! Nicole made a thousand dollars that night, gave it all to me, and made me her pimp! Taught me how to give oral sex and gave me my first ever blowjob. I had arrived. She had to turn herself in to do five years within sixty days. But she wanted to dress me like a pimp! Got my hair done like super fly. It was on!

My daddy's brother, Uncle Nelson, had a body shop on Manchester and Avalon. I bought a Buick "deuce in a quarter" Electra 225. It was green. I had it painted money green with metallic-green paint by Earl Shied for $69.99! It had power steering and a moonroof! I put on the gangster white walls. I was now looking like a real pimp with the brim hats and Boston leanies and Pierre Cardin dress shoe! The Mack!

Digging the scene in a gangster lean! Plus, I was still working as a busboy during the day and DJing and pimping during the night! Met a White girl named Tonya at a bus stop on Imperial and Central. She was a runaway from home, from Texas, and living with this bully in Watts! I took her to get her clothes from him, and she chose me as her pimp. My first one! She was good but jealous! I picked up this Native American girl named Tee Tee! She was from New York, young and so fine. I wanted her only for myself! Never really sent her out. Then I knocked Brenda, and now I was three-deep! Quit my job and started to learn the game of the pimps! Hooked up with this guy named Tipsy, who used to pay me to watch his hooker Marie. Plus, she would sneak and give me free sex anyway! Tipsy taught me more game. Until one night, we were in the La Brea Motel on La Brea and Slauson! It was these two sisters out of New Jersey. They were considered outlaws and wouldn't choose up!

So Tipsy told me, "This is what you do to outlaw hookers!" He put a pillow over her head and shot her!

We all left the motel! That fucked me up, and Tipsy heard I was snitching on him. He put the word out that he was looking for me. I called my father in Flint, Michigan, and told him the story. He sent me a plane ticket! The same day, he took me to his job at General Motors engine! While I was filling out the application, he snatched it out of my hands, took it to the back, and told his boss to hire me. And the next day, I was working. Couldn't believe my eyes!

PRESTON ALFONSO SCOTT, SR.

The first time I met my dad, I was thirteen years old. My mom had sent me to live with him, hoping he could straighten me out. We clashed! He and my stepmom, Ain't Lady. That was what all my cousins called her, and so did I! They were alcoholics, and they fought like cats and dogs! I only lasted two months! Ran away from home and was picked up for breaking in a gas station with a friend I had met in the school my dad had enrolled me in! The courts sent me back home to live with my mama! Six years later, my dad redeemed himself! Got me that job at GM and let me live with him and Ain't Lady! After I spent three months of living with them, they were still alcoholics.

I lived in a house with Barbara; she was twelve years older than me at thirty-two years old! After six months on the job, we could get a signature loan and buy any brand-new car off of a GM locks. This was 1977, and I bought 1976 Cadillac Coupe de Ville! It only had ten thousand miles on it, and it still had the seal or the smell of brand-new! It was creamy yellow with beige seat, all electric. I was a youngster and had this thing-player, pimp habit in me. So Barbara caught me messing around. We broke up! We worked on the assembly line together. Boy, was she jealous. She could not stand to see other women talk to me. She stabbed me on the job with a fingernail clip! I had to move to another job!

The '70s was good for Black folks and women of all colors! Women moved the crowds for equal rights, and they won and took off! Black folks started getting jobs. Life was good! So let's celebrate!! GM paid good money back then, and everybody in our twenties was driving brand-new cars! I hit the club scene; boy, I loved to dance! Every club I went to, I turned it out. Met a DJ named Harry "D." We hooked up, and I called myself Scottie "Bee" The Stinger! We were the tag team Dorall. I drove the '76 Coupe de Ville; he had the first ever 77 Lincoln Mark V! We both wore derby (player hats). If I wasn't DJing, then I moved the crowd with my pop-locking dance moves! Songs like "No Parking on the Dance Floor," "Take Your Dead Ass Home," "The Roof Is on Fire," and "The Roach Is on the Wall"! Parliament was out with "Flash Lights" and "Under Water Boogie," just to name a few!

ALL CRACKED UP

Women, oh yeah. I was now legally twenty-one years old! In 1979, I met Patricia, drop-dead super fine. So fine I lost my mind! I was so jealous of her pretty ass! I, the ex-pimp and boss player, fell in love. We had a son. She name him Ricky! We had broken up before he was born. I joined the army to straighten out my life! Asked her to wait for me; she didn't! Lost my job at GM because of jealousy of her! Left my job to try and catch her cheating; she was dating this married man before she met me! Got fired, move back to Oklahoma, and went to Fort Dix, New Jersey, in October 1979. Had met another redbone, Tina, and got her pregnant. But she waited for me. We left Muskogee in my red 1968 Chevy Impala, candy apple red with flakes and spoke rims! It was clean. We drove to Los Angeles, just her and I with our unborn child, pulling a U-Haul trailer with our belongings! Our daughter came early, breech, feet first instead of headfirst! They told us the road trip may have caused her to come early. I blamed myself; she could fit in the palm of my hand. I named her Shafonda Renae Scott! She died after six weeks of living at Martin Luther King Hospital in Watts! We buried her at Evergreen Cemetery in Inglewood in a small-ass box! That crushed our hearts! So we planned and had a son. I named him after me. He was born in March 1982 in Long Beach Memorial Hospital! Life was good; I drove for RTD—Rough, Tough, and Dangerous—city bus line number 55!

We lived in Long Beach on Twenty-First and Pine! Mostly all-White neighborhood. The Reigly District, they call it! I went to Rosston Barber College, worked at Harvey and Norris Barbershop in Lynwood part-time, and still drove the bus. Money was flowing fast and good. Then crack hit the scene. I was a straight square, L-seven. Didn't drink or smoke—nothing! But I loved oral sex! Tina hated giving it to me, so she would really give me $40 and tell me to hit the streets and let those hookers do it! It was on! My wife didn't mind! I was hurt and happy at the same time.

Remember Darlene? Oh yeah, eight years later, they hit my job, the sheriff, with a subpoena for child support. I have a daughter named Meca. I'd seen her picture and took a blood test, and I came back positive to be her father! They garnished my checks! Money started getting short. So I hit the drug scene! Started delivering drugs on Greyhound with my military uniform on with a duffel bag full of keys! Kilo's ten at a time; my cut was $2,000 a bird (kilo). I took ten at a time. I was still in the army, summer camp, and weekend warrior! Still driving for RTD and working at the barbershop. Bought myself a 1979 Chevy van, a 1978 Chevy Rally Sport, a 1971 Mercedes-Benz, and 1979 Volkswagen Rabbit convertible. Gave Tina the Benz for work; she was a manager at Save On Super Market. My van was my sex machine! Sex was out of control for me. Driving the bus, I picked up females all day long. Had plenty of money and paid for a lot of oral sex on the back of the bus. Was addicted to oral sex; it was better than getting pussy! Here I go. Oh yeah! At my barbershop, I would give up free Jheri curls for pussy and head, Norris and Harvey and I! We had a room at the back of the barbershop—our ho office, you could call it. I needed endurance; I couldn't keep up! Then my partners from RTD came by my house! They smoked crack cocaine, tried to give me some, and told it would help me fuck the shit out of women. I told them never. I was to cool for that!

Then one day at Veteran Park in Long Beach where I often played pickup basketball with the homies! There they were—Brenda and Smokey! Both jet black and pretty as all outdoors! Had Robert with me; he always helped me get women's attention and would tell on me to his mama!

So I asked them, "Could my son play with the little girls while I played ball?"

They agreed! After the games, they wanted a ride home and asked me if I got high! I lied and said yes. Bad mistake! It cost me my present and future right as I speak. Didn't know it back then! We dropped our kids off, got back into the van, and went to purchase drugs. I asked them how much; they said fifty bucks! So I asked if we could do sex. They agreed! I was thinking what kind of weed would cost fifty bucks! They came back with crack! They were in the back of my van, rocking it up. Now I'd seen my friends smoking the stuff. And I remembered them telling me I could fuck forever! I wanted to fuck the shit outta both of them. So yeah, I tried it, and they turned me upside down and in and out! Sex would never be the same again!

I went buck wild. They licked me like a lollipop from head to toe! Oh, wee! I even took some home and shared it with Tina! We both liked it and had great sex together! It had gotten so good until I didn't want to have sex without it! I had crack fever, hooked, but didn't realize it at the time. Ended up getting fired from RTD. Didn't reenlist for the military. The barbershop was all that existed! Bank account got lower. Started selling jewelry and things from my house. Then Tina left me, took our son, and moved back to Oklahoma! I was supposed to leave with them! Rented a U-Haul truck, went to get our furnisher, but never made it! On my way to pick up my family to move to Oklahoma, and get away from the drugs and all the drama, there she was, right at the freeway entrance with a see-through white dress on, jet black and pretty as all get-out! Picked her up. Had $500.00 dollars in my pocket! Told myself, *Just one more time. Twenty minutes at most. Spend only twenty bucks. Fuck her and get back to my family.* Yeah, right! Never made it! Sold all the furniture and even the U-Haul truck. It was over.

All bad train wreck, head on wreck, I flew over the cuckoo's nest! Lost everything! Busted, disgusted, and couldn't be trusted! I was all the way cracked the fucked up! Nothing could save me all the way up!

Here is how the name Peekaboo came about. In the early '80s, when I was balling and having mad money, I would go to Charlie and the Music Staff bikini bars! Both located on Florence Avenue, one on Figueroa and the other on Crenshaw Boulevard! Now if you sit at the back end on the dance floor, you could get a peek at the pussy if your money was right! And I had extra to play with! I would step in those spots either with my RTD uniform or my military uniform. And the girls knew I spent money. And they knew I paid to look, so yeah, they started calling me Peekaboo! It stuck with me now until this very day! Now let me explain another reason why. Get this! I started selling crack and hit the Hollywood scene. Ran into a couple of my pimp partners from back in my Inglewood days! I was driving up Western Avenue, crossing Santa Monica Boulevard. Didn't know at the time it was a ho boulevard for transgenders. Picked up what I thought was a pretty young Black girl! She wanted twenty bucks to give me oral sex, right up my alley. But I wanted to fuck her fine ass. She told me she was on her period. I told her I didn't care; I would use a condom. We wrestled, and I snatched away her Kotex. And it was peeka-woo, not boo! I beat his ass! Ever since then, I asked to see the pussy before we got a room! You really couldn't tell the difference.

I caught my first drug case in Hollywood, went to jail, and was put on probation. At the age of thirty-two years old, first time ever doing time in the county jail except for back in the early '70s, a few days here and there! I got a county lid one year, and I did about four months on it! Met Carl at the glasshouse. He asked me to call his Auntie Mama Gwyen. She lived in schoolyard hood off of Stelma and Rimpan! When I got out of jail, I moved in with her! Washington and La Brea was up the street, and it was the hookers' boulevard! And Gwyen's daughter Juicese worked as a hooker up there, my stepdaughter and my best friend. Never had sex with her; always wanted to. But I respected Mama Gwyen, and so did all the women in the neighborhood. If they found out I was her man, they would be afraid to get high with me and have sex. Gwyen would find out and beat their ass. Oh yeah, and mine too! (Smiles.) I enjoyed the makeup sex!

So one day, she found out I got high and fucked her best friend, Marie. She threw hot grease on me; I took off my shirt just in time to keep it from burning all the way through to my skin. But I did get burned! She called the police and told them I beat her up, and off to jail I went! She came to court and told them she lied! The DA didn't believe her; she was crying. They dropped the charges but violated my probation! Sentenced me to sixteen months in state prison in 1989. First time in prison, and it wouldn't be the last!

Back in 1986, I took a one-year leave of absence from RTD to try and get my wife Tina and Robert back. It didn't work, but I met Ronda and remembered her from high school. She was a cheerleader back then and wouldn't give me the time of the day! We hooked up; she was single with two kids, a girl and a boy. I moved to Oklahoma City with her. We had a daughter and got married in a church in Norman, Oklahoma, sooner she smoked weed! She snickered weed and cigarette, and I couldn't stand either. I told her I used to smoke crack; she said she did too! So we got high! Bad this club where we used to buy drugs to so after the marriage! We ended up selling her brother's ring that he let me used for our wedding. We went the next morning to this pawnshop stall to replace the one we sold! Got away with it. Went back the next day to get mine, and we got busted. Next day, went to court handcuffed to my wife and so embarrassed! Her parents had a home and a church, so they bailed her out but left me to rot! In the church we got married at, one of the deacons put up their house and bailed me out. I got probation!

Left there and went to Flint, Michigan. Wanted to meet my son Ricky. I did! Met a lady at Arby's. She invited me to church, so I went with her. She took me home with her. Didn't know where to go! So I stayed with her. We kept it a secret from the church because she was an evangelist! We got busted. We had to go before the church committee and confess our sins! Sister Jenifer told me it was okay if we had oral sex, but I couldn't penetrate her. Yeah, right. She was ten years older than me but had body to kill for! I slipped it on her; and she went crazy, saying we got to get married, we must pray, and we can't tell anybody. She was in love and convinced that God had sent me to her. But after confessing our sins to the committee, which she denied, she hated me! I had just gave my life over to the Lord and thought I was doing the right thing! They made me a deacon! Gave me the keys to the church and moved me in the church apartment next door! I drove the church van, and it was on—except that demon for sex. And all the single women were on me, getting in the van with dresses on with no panties and talking about "Help me, Brother Scott"; and I did. They would invite me over for dinner, and when I arrived, they would come to the door half-naked. I got weak in the knee! Then the word got out that I was doing the whole church. They took my deacon position, and I relapsed! I left the church, and I left God. But God never left me. As you read on through my story, you will soon learn why I praise and thank God for not leaving me!

Went back to LA. On the way back, stopped through Norman, Oklahoma, to see my baby girl Kathy. Even though Ronda had told me she got an abortion, the pastor of the church told me differently. Yeah, he was right. Ronda had my beautiful baby girl, and I was so proud but unhappy! I was running on probation and didn't and couldn't stay and end up back in Oklahoma City state prison! Spent about a week with Ronda and Kathy. Keisha and Justin bought my babe her babe bed, swing, Pampers, etc. Made love to Ronda, my wife, for the very last time. She cried and begged me to stay. Keisha and Justin, they all were crying with their mother, upstairs in the window, watching me leave in the pouring-down rain. Ronda was holding my baby girl. I couldn't look back; I just had to leave. Didn't wanna get locked back up! "Oh my dick," let me explain why! My mind keeps telling me no, but my dick keeps telling me yeah!

I'm not gay, but the guy sucking my dick certainly was! "Oh my dick" let me explain why! 1990 in Hollywood caught my second dope sells! Was sentenced to another sixteen months with half in state prison. Fought my case in HOJI—Hall of Justice! __ It's closed down now. They had a tunnel that you could walk through, straight to the courthouse! During booking process, met this guy named Harry. Every time they called my name, they would call his name also! Processing was mad as hell—drawing your blood, spraying you with powder, and, oh yeah, cracking a smile and looking up our ass. I could have sworn most of those deputies were gay, they halla open up wider, not that wide enough; and if you didn't, you would get the flashlight treatment. That's a whole another different story.

So Harry said to me, "You, you wanna do some easy time?"
I said, "Hell yeah."
"When we get to classification, tell them you gay."
I said, "Hell no, nigga. You wanna fight!"
Being called gay was fighting words when you were on the main line in LA County Jail, which housed over twenty thousand inmates! It was a real city; we were allowed to have cash money! And believe me, you could buy anything that your money can afford. They even had female staff that would sell you some pussy! That's another story! Yeah, "oh my dick"!

So I went along with Harry's suggestions. Said I was gay. Harry said they did another classification over there at HOJI! And you could tell you were straight; and they would keep you there and, the next day, send you to the fifteenth floor and make you a trustee. It worked. Let the fun begin (oh my dick). Now on the fourteenth and fifteenth floor, that's where they kept all the gay inmates. Remember I told the story about the one I picked up in Hollywood? Man, I'm not gay. But this was a place where most of them were queens, make you wanna throw your woman off the train. Yeah, oh my dick. It took three days to get to classification, and I was in the cell with one of those queens. She-he had grease on his/her shiny lips. I had remembered how good it was when the one in Hollywood had sucked my dick. So that night, I played sleep. Oh yeah, once again, oh my dick.

I got declassed, but on the down-low, I didn't wanna leave. In jail, the missing thing was sex, and now I know what a woman feels like and goes through! Me and Harry were hot items to them, and they even would fight over who was gonna suck our dicks next! "Oh my dick!" Needless to say, well, we gave our dicks a hell of a party! So when we got to the trustee dorm, we were dressed with gay jumpsuit on. Now we had to explain why. So Harry had already told me on what to say, that we made the deputies at classification mad so they sent us to the gay dorm!

The fellow said, "Yeah, right."

But they knew if they called us punks, those were fighting words. And both Harry and I were in top shape! And me, I loved to fight! I gave them that look, like "Make my day, and I wish you would." Back to that old saying, I'm not gay, but the guy sucking my dick was surely gay! (Smiles.) Now remember, I got turned out on crack getting my dick sucked! Yeah, I wouldn't have it any other way. Get your dick sucked while hitting the pipe, rubbing, and looking at some pussy. (Oh my dick!)

They sent me to Chino State Prison, and if you ever took psych meds, they would send you to Burtch Hall! They housed keep-aways, gay inmates, and triple CMs. I was CM, short for J Cats on psych meds! And they would house you with anybody. So yeah, they racked the gate and put me in the cell with one that looked like Janet Jackson. (Oh my dick.) She-he had a boyfriend! That night I played sleep again. "Ooh, wee." So we went to the yard for recreation. She-he didn't wanna move out of the cell with me. Well, laid the yard down! He thought he could fight. Yeah, right. I had to protect my manhood. He didn't have a chance; we went to the hole! We got out; she-he was with someone else! They tried to put me in the cell with another one. She-he was about six feet, four inches tall and looked like Queen Kong, an ape for real!

Said, "Hi, my name Lakeisha."

I was like "Hell no, I'm not going in the cell with that ugly motherfucker."

So back to the hole I go! Now I heard rumors that those type of she-hes would take your dick and your booty too!

Wasn't trying to play sleep with that big, ugly mother fucker. Hell to the no all! Got sent to Soladad State Prison and hit the yard, and there was a she-he named Dawn from Oakland! As fine as any runway model you have ever seen. At dinner time, you could see guys with their laundry bags full of canteen, running to get head, paying for it with canteen, and trying to finish before everybody got back from chow! They even busted the coach employee for smoking crack with Dawn in the gym! His wife was a fine-ass CO; and they walked him off the yard in front of her, and Dawn held yard in handcuffs, holding the crack pipe high in the air so everybody could see! Dawn was handcuffed right with him.

Went back to Mama Gwyen, she had lost her apartment. We ended up on Skid Row. Peekaboo, here we go! She went to a women's shelter. Parole put me in the Frontier Hotel on Fifth and Pain—I mean, Main! (Smiles.) The hotel was all cracked up! Rooms tore up! Twelve floors. You could start from the first floor and try to make it to the eleventh floor. That's where they housed us parolees! If the elevator didn't work, you had to walk. Peekaboo on the way up the steps. Women were hanging out with miniskirts on with no panties! And as you were walking your way up, you could see nothing but pussy on every floor! Peekaboo, it was hard making it to the eleventh floor! And of course, you could smoke crack and get your dick sucked right there on the stairways; and if you wanted to fuck, they had at least four hallway restrooms. You had to wait your turn for a stall. Or sit her up on the sink! All these things were acceptable in all the Skid Row hotels back then—the Cecil Hotel, Alexandria Hotel, Rosslyn Hotel, and Huntington Hotel. Don't mention the SROs!

ALL CRACKED UP

Single room occupancy! Skid Row. Everything goes, and I jumped right in.

Got my third sell case. It was for selling of leiu of, the court's term for bunk dope. I had learn how to rock up BC Powder and papern for women's period. It looked better than dope! Used to be a DA reject. Then they came up with this law for bunk dope. One day, on Santa Monica and Highland, I had to get off at Sunset and had to hide from the one I sold bunk dope too! A guy pulled up on me butt naked and offered me $500.00 dollar cash to look at my chest while he jacked off. I took the money and ran. Remember, I used to be a pimp! My girls told me stories. So now I took off my shirt, and boy, did they pull over! I was built like our Governor Arnold, lifting weights in prison. I was a beast, jumping in cars, getting the gay folks' money, and jumping out. Easy money, right? Hell no! Until one day, it was a sting operation, and I went to jail for prostitution. Now how in the hell was I going to explain that! Tried to jump outta the car with the money, and police came from everywhere! Peeka-woo!

I was sick, went to court, and got time served, and now it's on my jacket. Hell to the no all! But the money was so easy; gay people are soft as cotton, scarier than real women! It wasn't robbery or nothing! You got tricked, never worried about them coming back wanting to fight. Sometimes they would come back and throw ice or apple at me and were calling me nigga! Oh, well, the money was good.

Then one night, I jumped in the car with the devil! Yeah, he had a trick for me! Gave me fifty bucks, and I went to jump out the car. He hit the automatic lock button. And I turned around and faced with a .357 chrome-plated pistol grip handle, and yeah, that's a different story!

Back to HOJI, it had gotten even worse. We could walk up and down the stairwells with no escorts. From school, chow, library, church, etc.; and you would see men exchanging jumpsuits with the she-hes and getting their dick sucked on the steps!

The deputies would yell, "Get your dick out that man's mouth!"

I think they enjoyed catching us too. Free live porn. Jailhouse rock! "Oh my dick!" They didn't do count until ten o'clock at night; so you would see inmates going to church and exchanging jumpsuits in the stairwells. So that everybody would make it back on time for count! The deputies weren't tripping as long as it kept the peace and made their job easier! Then I was sent to Wasco State Prison in 1993, and it was a she-he named Keisha that hit the yard with some shorts made like women biker shorts! And Keisha had ass that shook like jelly. I'm not gay, but damn, this Keisha rocked the whole yard. They called Keisha over the loudspeaker and told Keisha to take it back in and take off those shorts! Keisha almost started a riot between the Crips and the Bloods. The Bloods ended up with Keisha! So, ladies, if you are in doubt about the down-low, yeah, you might wanna keep your man away from your gay friends, especially if he has been to prison!

So now I'm well-known on Skid Row, in and out of jail and prison! Every man wants sex when they get out of jail. What's that song? "What you gonna do when you get outta jail? I'm gonna have some fun." What do I consider fun? Well, fun to me is when I cum! "Oh my dick!" That's how crack cocaine had controlled my life for the past thirty years! From 1989 to now 2019! Been a cum freak all my life, so crack is not the only addiction that I have! I'm also addicted to sexual pleasure and any way that I can get it! God has blessed me that I haven't caught AIDS! I rarely used condoms when I traded drugs for sex.

There was a coach that came through the county jail, and he would show films on people with AIDS. I mean ugly sores, bumps, scars, rapse, etc.! And that's another reason I played peekaboo! If I'd seen any of those signs on your pussy or body, yeah, it was peeka-woo and shame on you. I'm outta here. My high would come down real fast! Through all the times I've been drug by cars, hit in the head with car jacks and two-by-four wood, and shot in the head, God has still kept me from killing myself and not getting life in prison. Yeah, now you can really see how I'm all cracked up. Been in countless rehabs through the VA. Back in 1979, my drill sergeant beat me and traumatized me! Yeah, that's a different story! I pray daily and ask God for forgiveness and thank him for my life and his grace! Made up my own church song, "Hear my prayer, oh Lord. Hear my prayer, oh

Lord. All I ask in return for glorifying your name is that you hear my prayers, oh Lord! Thank you, Lord!"

I'm in hopes that my book will open up the eye of the public in the world around us, about the addiction to crack cocaine and other drug that used, and that human beings especially addicted to drugs are not bad people but only make bad choices while under their addiction to whatever their drug of choice is. Understand in life that we all shall experience some trauma or turmoil in our lives. But no man nor woman in God's great earth has the power to judge and condemn than our great holy God! He is just and merciful all the way to the end of our lives!

I'm now sixty-two years old and have written this book in five days in CTC 3, West Room 7-LA, Twin Towers! Sixty-two years old is retirement age; the past thirty years of my life, I've been in and out of jail! Had so many different kids—by Darlene, my daughter Meca, forty-one yrs. old; Patricia, my son Ricky, thirty-nine years old; and Robert with his mother, Tina. He is thirty-seven years old. They all know each other. I thank God for that. Meca has given me five wonderful grandkids, and my grandson alike has given me three beautiful great-granddaughters! Haven't met them yet but have seen and talked to them through Facebook. I'm so proud of each of them! While in Fort Dix, New Jersey, I got a girl pregnant and can't remember the name. Darcell Robinson gave birth to me a daughter in 1993. Her name is Breonty, born in Oklahoma City! I and Darcell met in LA! Transferred my parole to Muskogee and remember, I was on the run as soon as I got there in 1986. They locked me up! Found out that my daughter had been put in child custody because me and Darcell were on crack cocaine. Faye Foley told me she gave birth to some twins, boy and girl! Just heard one of them, the boy, took his own life! Never met them. They should have been about forty years old! I am in hopes that this book will gross enough money whereas I won't have to steal anymore! Find a way to meet and rejoice with all my children together that they may meet their true father, and we shall all get to know and love one another! This is my story about being all cracked up!

To be continued in my next book!

PUT AN HICKIE ON MY BOOTY!

Skid Row—the lifestyle of the poor and unfamous! Couldn't tell us that! Three missions! The LA, the Union, and, oh yeah, my favorite, the Midnight Mission! It's called that for a reason. Midnight Mission was on the corner of Sixth and San Pedro. Anything goes! And I do mean anything—twenty-four-hour outdoor sleeping and restroom facilities! Oh my dick! The restrooms, you could smoke crack, shoot dope, etc.! Then look for the loneliest and broke-ass female addict that would give you the time of your life; and, get this, it could all be paid for—at the cost of twenty bucks! Yeah, ladies, what do you want to do? The drug-addict ladies. Yeah, us men, we can get it all night long for a dove! Slang for twenty bucks 'cause, in my world, it's only you. What you want to do for my love, I'll get it done for a dove!

TENT CITY

The tents on Skid Row were like a poor man's Motel 6! You could rent a tent out for five bucks for two hours or until you smoked up all your crack. The owner of the tent now became a bodyguard. He, or she, would faithfully sit out in front of their tent and make sure no one bothers you, as long as you share your crack with them too! And if you didn't wanna get set up for a jack move or robbery, yeah, that would be the smartest thing for you to do! Unless, you're like me; I was well known! Being well known in Skid Row basically kept you from being a victim of Skid Row! And it gave you the street power to do mostly whatever you want as long as you didn't get too far outta control. You would have the free will to smoke and sell crack to support your habit basically on any block that you want, except Cubans' corner! Yeah, the Cubans fought and killed for their corner; and they had it. But they also were __ only to sell on that corner! South siders try to take over some blocks.

But in Skid Row, we had formed what we called DTGs—Downtown Gangsters! It consisted of Black gangs from every known gang throughout Southern California! Yeah, and we all stuck together! Wasn't any set trippin'. Sure, we had our problems, but we weren't having any South siders take our poor Hollywood from us. Yeah, anything goes! You could get a lap dance nude in broad daylight and get your dick sucked on any corner in broad daylight. Just put a jacket over her head, and nobody would say anything, not even the police. Most of us had seen it all, and yeah we learned to mind our own business! Because most people on Skid Row, once you become all cracked up, you don't get nothing and don't want nothing. So yeah, you become part of that lifestyle of the poor and unfamous.

PRESTON ALFONSO SCOTT, SR.

I can remember being in an alley, smoking crack with one of my many super head friends. Yeah, you get to know that one female who loves to smoke crack and suck your dick to death! You literally have to damn near have to make her stop. Yeah, oh my dick! It started to pour down and rain. A guy passed through the alley with a piece of an umbrella. I gave him a piece of my crack for it. I and my female friend got asshole naked. Put our wet clothes on the ground, and as I hit the crack pipe, she got on her knees and sucked my dick for a minute. Then she bent over, and I fucked her from behind. After we finished, we laughed and began to sing that famous song "In the Rain." It may sound crazy! Yeah, that was the best sex while being high that I have ever had—in broad daylight! That's what happens when you are "all cracked up"!

The side effects to all of this lead you to LA County jail and Twin Towers and eventually to state prison. Yeah, that's another story.

The end!

MY DICK HAS A BRAIN

Let me explain. As my journey continued, I was up in San Francisco. I met this beautiful young girl, fine as all get-out. But when I took her to the motel, she got naked. I'd seen these red bumps all over her body. I remembered those red bumps from watching a film on AIDS! So I asked her if she had AIDS. She began to cry. Remember, I am a mother's boy. The thought came to my mind—she is somebody's mother and daughter! Then she began to cry, and she begged me not to leave.

"Please have sex with me."

I began to cry, then I called on the name of the Lord. *God, please be with me.*

I lay with her, and I felt her pain. I stayed with her all night, and we made love and cried together.

I told her, "God loves you."

As my journey continued, seemed like all I would do was to out the alley under the freeways. Then I would start to be attracted to those women who were dirty and smell of urine. I would invite them to a motel and tell them they could take a shower. And I would buy them a dove.

Then I would ask them, "What happened to you? Why you don't care about yourself?"

And they all would tell me they were either beaten by a man or raped by a man. The same thing that happened to my mother. Even though I got high with them, I felt like they needed to be loved and to feel good about themselves and that all men are not like that. Plus, "God loves you, and I love you too!"

As my journey continued, I would be thinking with my dick, looking in these alleys at three to four o'clock in the morning. Couldn't find no nice-looking girls. Didn't have enough money to afford a motel or pay for a hooker! I walked up on this woman. She was in the alley up under a blanket, dirty and nasty. I went up under the blanket with her.

She kept saying, "No, go away."

I told her, "I didn't care about you being dirty or nasty. I'm dirty and nasty too."

She began to laugh. We got high, and we laughed.

I told her, "God loves you, and I love you too."

Then as my journey continued, I met this lady that slept on this bus stop. She was fat and unattractive. But for some reason, I could see the beauty in her. So I sat at the bus stop with her.

People would drive by in their cars and walk by laughing and saying, "You would lay down with anything."

But I continued to get her high and lay with her on that bus stop. And I told her, "God loves you, and I love you too."

Now that I think back on my sexual addiction, I was being "I wanna fuck everything I see, especially if she has a shirt on." Back in 1986, I gave my life over to the Lord and was baptized through the blood over the Spirit and was cleansed of my sin. But why couldn't I get clean off these damn drugs?

Then I began to ask God, *Is this my journey? Do you want me to seek out those women who are lost and unwanted?*

Then I began to pray and ask God to be with me. Somehow I believed God put my brain in my dick, not for sexual pleasures, but to somehow touch the heart and souls of those women who are lost and trapped in their misery in being beaten and raped and abused or molested by their uncles or fathers, because I have met and laid with women who have been through all that. God's message through this book and my journey is to let men in this world realize that, if you have a mother and daughters, then stop abusing these women that we say we love. I was a protector of my mama! These women out there—lost, battered, and abused—are some man's daughter. And I know there is no man on God's great planet who would want their mother or daughter to be treated like that.

In the same church that I got baptized in, they gave me an apartment next to the church. And I remembered that I left; God never left me. God uses us in many ways and fashion to deliver the message—that every man and woman shall bow and kneel and confess that the Lord is the one and only as our creator who will continue to use us in countless ways that you can imagine. Men, love the women as if you would have that same love for your mother or daughter! 'Cause remember, there is a man out there somewhere who wouldn't stand for you to treat their mother or daughter like that. May God help us all. I've tested for AIDS and never been positive!

It's funny that men would tell me that I was a sucker, a real trick! But I would tell them, "They desire all my money for putting up with my sexual pleasure. Why would you feel like that? The thing that they be asked to do, in their addiction, that we as men don't care nothing about. I paid them because they deserve it. I wanna give them all money in hopes that they will do something positive for themselves for putting up with our sick addiction habits!"

There is one more child of God left. She has been beaten and had her teeth knocked out, and she is tuck in Skid Row. They have her birth certificate. She said it cost $1,500.00 to get it back. She is trying to hustle, the Skid Row way. And she have gotten involved with a man who continues to beat her. I'm in love with her, but I'm much older than her. She is thirty-three years old; I'm sixty-two years old. Her father is fifty-six! She is from the island. She is Black and so beautiful. She was married to a famous fighter who abused her, and it led her to the women's shelter downtown! I met her at a mission on Skid Row. She had tears in her eyes. But I could feel the pain that she suffered from! I could hear her heartbeat in fear. She needs a place to lie down and go to sleep. I ran to my room and took the blankets off my bed so that she could go to sleep. Through this book, I hope to be able to get her smile back and her hopes and dreams back. She even talks about killing herself. She graduated from USC and has a bachelor's degree. But her pride won't let her family help her. Because of my pride, it took me thirty years, in and out of prisons and jails, to realize that I was all cracked up. I asked God to bless this story so that I can help her and other women who have been beaten and battered as my mother was. It's just truly hard for me to see her throw her life away and end up like me and becoming all cracked!

The women, mothers, and daughters on Skid Row, they get used, laughed at, and treated like tramps. It's not by choice. These women have been beaten and batted and broken until they, too, have got all cracked up!

My God bless all the women of the world, whom we men come from through birth. How can you beat your own mother!

This book is to honor our Heavenly Father, the Creator of the universe! Heed to the message! Written by a momma's boy who became all cracked up!

ABOUT THE AUTHOR

Preston Alfonso Scott, Sr. tried twenty drug programs, but it wasn't to. He fell to his knees and cried out to God to take the demon from him! Since then, he's been clear and clean of crack cocaine! He's just a small-time country boy from Muskogee, Oklahoma.

"In OUR Father's house... in Heaven!"

Our Precious Angels...
"Took Flight, February 2, 2021"

www.ingramcontent.com/pod-product-compliance
Lightning Source LLC
Chambersburg PA
CBHW031659040426
42453CB00006B/348